Heroes of History

REBELS

Written by Anita Ganeri
Illustrated by Joe Todd Stanton

PowerKiDS press

Published in 2026 by The Rosen Publishing Group, Inc.
2544 Clinton Street, Buffalo, NY 14224

Created by:
Author: Anita Ganeri
Additional text: Nicola Barber
Illustrator: Joe Todd Stanton
Additional Illustrations: Katie Abey
Editorial: Hannah Wilson, Lydia Halliday
Senior Designer: Krina Patel
Designer: Natasha Rees
Index: Vanessa Bird

Cataloging-in-Publication Data

Names: Ganeri, Anita, 1961, author. | Todd-Stanton, Joe, illustrator.

Title: Rebels / by Anita Ganeri, illustrated by Joe Todd-Stanton.

Description: Buffalo, NY : PowerKids Press, 2026. | Series: Heroes of history | Includes glossary and index.

Identifiers: ISBN 9781499454901 (pbk.) | ISBN 9781499454918 (library bound) | ISBN 9781499454925 (ebook)

Subjects: LCSH: Dissenters--Biography--Juvenile literature. | Social reformers--Biography--Juvenile literature. | Political activists--Biography--Juvenile literature.

Classification: LCC HN13.G364 2026 | DDC 303.48'40922--dc23

Manufactured in the United States of America

CPSIA Compliance Information: Batch #CSPK26. For further information contact Rosen Publishing at 1-800-237-9932.

CONTENTS

INTRODUCTION

History is packed with heroes and heroines who left a lasting legacy behind. Some were larger-than-life characters, born leaders who inspired their followers. Others worked away quietly, shunning the limelight. They earned their fame in different ways - through hard work, determination and, sometimes, sheer luck.

REBELS

Scattered throughout history are people who have stood out because they didn't fit in or conform. These rebellious spirits have led revolts against an established order that they considered unfair, and worked tirelessly for people who had no rights of their own. Often these rebels turned their own lives upside down to help others, and even risked being killed.

Martin Luther

Spartacus

But all had an unwavering belief that what they were doing was right, and this inspired them to carry on, even when the going got horribly tough.

In this chapter, you can read about a gladiator who led a slave revolt, a reformer who dared to question the way people worshipped, a woman who escaped slavery to lead other enslaved people to freedom, and a man who risked his life to save others from certain death.

Oskar Schindler

Harriet Tubman

SPARTACUS

Slave Leader

In the first century BCE, a daring gladiator defied the mighty Romans and escaped from his training school. He was soon joined by tens of thousands of other runaway enslaved people. For two years, Spartacus and his army kept the Romans at bay. Then their luck ran out.

Early years

We know very little about who Spartacus actually was. It is thought that he came from Thrace (modern-day Bulgaria) and may once have been a soldier in the Roman Army. He was later taken prisoner, possibly for deserting his post, and was sold as an enslaved person. Another story says that he was a prisoner of war, captured by the Romans.

Gladiator school

Because of his great strength, Spartacus was sold as a gladiator. He was sent to be trained at a ludus (gladiator school) near the town of Capua in Italy. The ludus was owned by a man called Lentulus Batiatus. Like all gladiator schools, it was strictly run and training was tough. Most gladiators had short brutal lives and were expected to fight only two or three times before they were killed. But they were also valuable commodities to their owners, and it was vital that they put on a good show to entertain the crowds.

There were different types of gladiators, with different types of armor and weapons. Spartacus was a murmillo. This heavyweight fighter carried a rectangular shield and a long sword, and wore a leather belt and arm guard. He also wore a large bronze helmet with a crest and ornate grille to protect his face. We don't know how good a gladiator Spartacus really was, but we do know that, one day, in 73 BCE, he decided he'd had enough of ludus life.

SPARTACUS' REBEL DIARY

Sometime in 73 BCE
Capua, Italy

We've made it out — about 70 of us — but only just. The ludus guards discovered our escape plan so we had to fight our way out with kitchen knives. Luckily, we also found a couple of wagons loaded with armor and weapons outside, so we grabbed the lot. Anyway, we're heading for Mount Vesuvius and, I'm told, hundreds of other slaves are also on their way.

Later in 73 BCE
Mount Vesuvius, Italy

Ha! That'll teach those Romans to mess with us. They sent Glaber (their military commander) and his men after us — most of the legions are away fighting, so it was the best they could do. Glaber's tactic was to sit and wait until we were starving and had to surrender. It never happened! We made some ropes from vines, climbed down the mountain and took the Romans by surprise!

Spring 72 BCE
Mount Garganus, Italy

We spent the winter in the south, training and arming our new recruits. There are about 70,000 of us now – slaves, gladiators, you name it. We'd begun our march north when disaster struck. Crixus (one of our leaders) had gone ahead, but the Romans tracked him down and killed him and thousands of his men. So, we took our revenge.

Sometime in 71 BCE
Straits of Messina

We were pushed further south by Crassus and his legions, but I had a cunning plan. I paid some pirates to take us over to Sicily where we could get reinforcements. Dirty rotten cheats. They stole our money, then sailed off, leaving us stranded on the beach. We need to head east – and fast – before Crassus catches us.

Later in 71 BCE
Campania, Italy

That's it – we're trapped. We're surrounded by Romans – Lucullus in front, Crassus behind, and Pompey to the north. We've forced the Romans to do a merry dance over the last two years, but there's no way out for us now. The only thing left to do is turn around and fight with all our might . . .

INSPIRING REBELS

Down the ages, brave individuals such as Spartacus have dared to challenge their masters, and have inspired others to follow them. And, like Spartacus, many died as a result of their actions.

A murmillo gladiator, like Spartacus

Inspired by Spartacus

Spartacus probably died in that final battle, but his body was never found. The Romans took terrible revenge on the survivors, crucifying 6,000 of them along the Appian Way from Rome to Capua. Spartacus inspired future rebels, and his story lives on in many books and films.

Toussaint Louverture

Toussaint was born into slavery on the French island colony of St. Domingue. In 1791, he helped organize a revolt against the French enslavers and later took control of the island. St. Domingue became the independent Republic of Haiti in 1804.

Toussaint Louverture, 1743–1803

Statue of Garibaldi in Italy

Giuseppe Garibaldi

Garibaldi became involved in a war between some of the small kingdoms that made up Italy, and was exiled to South America. His exploits there as a guerrilla fighter made him famous. He returned to Italy in 1848 and fought in battles that eventually led to the creation of a unified Italy in 1861.

Timeline of courageous rebels

72 BCE
Spartacus
Former gladiator leads a revolt against the Romans.

1381
Wat Tyler
Killed during his leadership of the unsuccessful Peasants' Revolt in England.

1791
Toussaint Louverture
Organizes a revolt as leader of the Haitian Revolution.

1857
Lakshmibai, Rani of Jhansi
Becomes a leading figure in the Indian Rebellion.

1861
Giuseppe Garibaldi
Italian patriot helps to create a united Italy.

MARTIN LUTHER

Religious Reformer

In 1517, German priest Martin Luther nailed a list on to a church door. The list of points strongly criticized the Roman Catholic Church and caused a sensation. It sparked the "Reformation" — one of the biggest changes in the history of the Christian Church.

Early life

Born on November 10, 1483, in Eisleben, Germany, Martin was the eldest son of a copper miner. He had several brothers and sisters. Martin's father, Hans, wanted the best for his family and was determined that Martin should become a laywer. He sent Martin to a school that taught Latin and philosophy – Martin hated his time there.

In 1501, aged 19, Martin enrolled at the University of Erfurt. It was another miserable time in his life. He was made to get up at four o'clock every morning and he found his studies boring. After receiving his degree, he signed up at the university law school, but dropped out almost at once. He was much more interested in theology than law.

Becoming a monk

On July 2, 1505, Martin was riding back to the university after a visit home. A storm broke out and a bolt of lightning struck close by. Martin was terrified, but took his survival as a sign from God and vowed to become a monk. Two weeks later, he left law school, sold his books, and entered an Augustinian friary (monastery). Over the next few years, he devoted himself to his calling, praying, fasting, and making pilgrimages and, in 1507, he was ordained as a priest. He was offered a post at the University of Wittenberg, teaching theology.

But Martin also began to question some of the practices of the Catholic Church that he thought were corrupt. He was especially angry about "indulgences." These were promises that the clergy sold to people, taking away any punishments for their sins.

MARTIN LUTHER'S REFORMATION DIARY

October 31, 1517
Wittenberg, Germany
I've written to the Bishop about the sale of indulgences. Something has got to be done. I've also sent him a copy of my "95 Theses," criticizing some of the other practices of the Church. For good measure, I've nailed another copy to the door of All Saints' Church. They won't like it, but there we are. Some friends have offered to translate them from Latin into German. Then we can get them printed so that people all over Europe can read them.

January 3, 1521
Wittenberg
Pope Leo has excommunicated (expelled) me from the Church and has banned the 95 Theses. Well, he did warn me, I suppose. He sent a letter telling me to take back some of the things I'd written, but I refused. I still stand by all of them, despite his threats. Then I set fire to the letter, in front of everyone.

April 1521
Wartburg Castle, Eisenbach
I was ordered to appear before the emperor at Worms, where they laid out copies of my writings on the table and asked me if I stood by them. I do! So, they've declared me a heretic and an outlaw. Luckily, I've still got some good friends. They've helped me to escape to Wartburg, where I'm in hiding in the castle. I've no idea how long I'll be here.

June 13, 1525
Wittenberg
A happy day. I'm back in Wittenberg, and today, Katharina and I got married. She used to be a nun, but I helped her to escape from her convent by smuggling her out in a barrel used for storing fish. We're moving into my old monastery — it was a wedding gift!

Sometime in 1534
Wittenberg
I've spent the last few years preaching, writing, and organizing our new Church. Many people can't read Latin so I've also translated the Bible into German, and it's being published today. It has been a long time coming — I started working on it while I was still in hiding. But if it means more people can read it, it's been worth all the hard work.

DEVOTED REFORMERS

Martin Luther changed Christianity forever when he broke away from the Roman Catholic Church. Here you can find out about other Christians who have had a major impact on their religion.

Statue of Martin Luther, Wittenberg

Luther's new church

Martin Luther's German Bible was popular and helped spread his ideas across Germany. From 1533, Martin was dean of theology at the University of Wittenberg, a center for the new Protestant Church. Before his death in 1546, he suffered from many (probably stress-related) illnesses.

John Calvin, 1509-1564

John Calvin

Calvin was interested in the ideas of the Reformation and, in 1536, published a statement of his Protestant beliefs. In 1538, he was forced to leave Geneva, Switzerland, because of his beliefs, but later returned to lead the city's Protestant movement.

A young Joseph Smith reading the Bible

Joseph Smith

American Joseph Smith said that he was visited by an angel called Moroni, who revealed golden plates inscribed with characters. Smith translated and, in 1830, published these characters as the Book of Mormon. The same year, Smith started a new church, but its members were persecuted.

Timeline of religious reformers

313 BCE

Constantine the Great

Roman Emperor issues the Edict of Milan, allowing Christians to worship freely in the Roman Empire.

1517

Martin Luther

Protestant reformer nails his list of protests against the Roman Catholic Church to a church door in Wittenberg.

1536

John Calvin

French reformer becomes a leading figure in the Protestant Reformation.

1738

John Wesley

English priest experiences a profound spiritual experience and founds Methodism with his brother Charles Wesley.

1830

Joseph Smith

American religious leader founds Mormonism and the Church of Jesus Christ of Latter-day Saints.

Harriet Tubman

Anti-slavery Activist

Born into slavery, Harriet Tubman made a daring escape. Then she devoted herself to rescuing other enslaved people – many of them friends and relatives – leading them to freedom along the Underground Railroad, away from the clutches of the slave-catchers.

Born into slavery

Harriet's parents, Ben Ross and Harriet Green, were born into slavery in Dorchester County, Maryland. They were owned by different masters, but got married in 1808, and had nine children. Harriet was born in about 1822 and was originally named Araminta, or "Minty" for short.

Harriet's mother tried hard to keep her family together, but three of her daughters were sold to a different master. She managed to save her youngest son by hiding him from the slave-traders. When Harriet was about five years old, she was hired out as a nursemaid. Her job was to look after the baby, and she was badly beaten if it woke up and cried.

Planning her escape

Over the next few years, Harriet was hired out many times to different masters. Once, she was sent to a store for supplies. Another enslaved person had gone to the store without his owner's approval and the master demanded that Harriet help him catch the man. When Harriet refused, the master threw a heavy metal weight at her head. As a result of her injury, she suffered fits and headaches for the rest of her life.

In 1844, Harriet married free man John Tubman. She also changed her name to Harriet. Then, in 1849, her master died. To pay off his debts, his widow was forced to sell enslaved people, including Harriet. Harriet did not wait to discover her fate. In September, she and her two brothers escaped, but her brothers had a change of heart and returned shortly after. Harriet saw them safely back and then set off alone.

HARRIET TUBMAN'S ANTI-SLAVERY DIARY

October 1849
Philadelphia, Pennsylvania
This time I set off on my own, travelling at night to give the slave-catchers the slip. Someone gave me the names of people and places on the Underground Railroad. (It's not a real railroad – the "tracks" are safe routes and the "stations" are safe places to shelter.) Now I'm in Pennsylvania, the free state. It feels like I'm in heaven. I keep looking at my hands to make sure I'm still the same person.

Sometime in 1854
Maryland
I'm back in Maryland where I'm helping more slaves to escape. I've been back many times since I left. At first, I was terrified of being caught, but I've got used to it now. And I've got a revolver. This time, I bought some chickens to make it look as if I was running an errand in town. When I saw an old master, I let the chickens go, so he looked at them, not me.

October 18, 1858
Harper's Ferry, Virginia

Captain John Brown asked me to help him start an uprising in the south. He wanted me to recruit slaves for a raid on Harper's Ferry to capture the weapons store. But it's all gone horribly wrong. John Brown's been arrested and tried for treason, but I know he wanted the best for us.

January 1862
Port Royal, South Carolina

I'm here in Port Royal, helping slaves who've run away from the Civil War fighting. They're free now, but they've nowhere to go. I've also been nursing the soldiers, dressing their wounds and making medicines from roots and plants. But money's tight so I've been making pies and root beer to sell to the troops.

June 2, 1863
Combahee River

Colonel Montgomery has been planning a raid on the Combahee River plantations to destroy the enemy supplies, and today was the day. My job was to guide three boatloads of men across so they could set fire to the farms. We also managed to rescue about 750 slaves. When they heard the boats were going back, they ran after us, clutching their belongings.

BRAVE ABOLITIONISTS

Harriet Tubman's bravery in returning time after time to the south to lead enslaved people to freedom was an inspiration for all abolitionists — people who spoke out against slavery.

Statue of Harriet Tubman

A long life

After the Civil War, Harriet remarried war veteran Nelson Davis (her former husband had stayed in Maryland). Despite her growing fame, Harriet remained poor — partly due to her generosity. In 1903, she donated land for the construction of a home for the aged. She died there in 1913.

Former enslaved people in Virginia, 1862

Olaudah Equiano

Born in Nigeria, Equiano was kidnapped as a child and taken to the British colony of Virginia where he was enslaved. He taught himself to read and write and, in 1767, bought his freedom and joined the abolitionist movement.

Abraham Lincoln, 1809-1865

Abraham Lincoln

In 1863, President Lincoln issued the Emancipation Proclamation, freeing all enslaved people in the Confederacy. This was followed by the 13th Amendment, abolishing slavery in the United States. Lincoln did not live to see the results of his work — he was assassinated in April 1865.

Timeline of anti-slavery activists

1789

Olaudah Equiano

Autobiography *The Interesting Narrative of the Life of Olaudah Equiano* is published, helping to turn British public opinion against slavery.

1833

William Wilberforce

English politician and the leader of the anti-slavery movement in Britain dies. Shortly after, slavery is abolished in the British Empire.

1849

Harriet Tubman

African-American abolitionist escapes from slavery and goes on to help many other enslaved people escape through the Underground Railroad.

1852

Harriet Beecher Stowe

American author and abolitionist publishes *Uncle Tom's Cabin*, a book about the impact of slavery.

1863

Abraham Lincoln

President Lincoln issues the Emancipation Proclamation, freeing all enslaved people in a group of southern states.

OSKAR SCHINDLER

Wartime Life-saver

During World War II, German businessman Oskar Schindler risked his life to save hundreds of Jews working in his factories. This was extraordinary enough – but Schindler also belonged to the Nazi Party, which was determined to destroy the Jews.

Early life

Oskar was born on April 28, 1908, into a German family in Moravia (modern Czech Republic). His father, Hans, owned a farm machinery business. After school, Oskar worked for Hans and enjoyed racing motorcyles.

In 1928, Oskar married Emilie Pelzl, the daughter of a wealthy farmer. The couple lived with Oskar's parents. Shortly afterwards, Oskar left his father's business and did a variety of jobs, including managing a driving school and working in a bank. He also joined the Czech army where he rose to the rank of Lance Corporal.

War work

In 1936, Schindler began working as a spy for the Abwehr, the Nazi intelligence service. His duties included collecting information on railways and the military, as well as recruiting other spies in preparation for Nazi invasions of other countries. In 1938, the Czech government arrested him for spying and put him in prison, but he was later released. He joined the Nazi Party the following year.

Following the German invasion of Poland in autumn 1939, the Schindlers moved to Krakow. Here, Oskar continued his work for the Abwehr, helped by his wife. In Krakow, homes and businesses owned by Polish Jews had been seized by the Nazis, and Oskar was able to buy a Jewish-owned enamelware factory called Rekord Ltd. He renamed it the Deutsche Emailwarenfabrik Oskar Schindler (German Enamelware Factory Oskar Schindler), or "Emalia" for short.

SCHINDLER'S WARTIME DIARY

August 1940
Krakow, Poland
The new factory's been open for a few months and everything's going well. We're making enamel pots and pans for the army. Let's hope it makes me lots of money in return. I've taken on a Jewish bookkeeper and some Jewish workers. I'll hire some more when we get busier.

June 1942
Krakow, Poland
I'd always known that the Nazis had started sending Jews to labor camps (where they'll most likely be killed). I've managed to keep my workers safe — for now — by bribing the officials with luxury goods I've smuggled in on the black market. And the factory's started making shells and ammunition so we can claim they're doing essential war work.

March 13, 1943
Krakow, Poland

A terrible day. The Nazis have burned down the ghetto and killed thousands of Jews in the streets. Thousands more are being sent to the concentration camp at Plaszow. I'd heard about the plans through my contacts, so I kept my workers at the factory overnight so they'd be safe. The Nazis want to move the factory inside the camp, but I'm going to try to persuade them to let me stay put and house the Jews at the factory instead.

October 1944
Brunnlitz, Czechoslovakia

The Nazis are sending more and more Jews to the camps, so I've had to take drastic action. I've managed to get permission to move my factory to Brunnlitz, where we'll be making anti-tank grenades. I've got to make a list of the Jewish workers I want to take with me — there'll be about 1,200 in total. I don't want to think what will happen to the rest.

May 7, 1945
Brunnlitz, Czechoslovakia

Germany has surrendered! The war is nearly over. We all gathered on the factory floor to listen to Winston Churchill (the British Prime Minister) announcing the news on the radio. I don't know what will happen to me now. I'm still, officially, a member of the Nazi Party so there's a very strong possibility I could be arrested.

DETERMINED NAZI OPPOSERS

Oskar Schindler survived the war, but many others who tried to resist the Nazis did not. You can find out here about a few of the brave people who refused to give in to the Nazi regime.

A German concentration camp

"Schindler's Jews"

After the war, Schindler was penniless — he'd spent all his money bribing the Nazis to spare his workers. But his bravery and determination had saved 1,200 lives. When he died in 1974, his funeral was attended by hundreds of "Schindler's Jews" — the people he had saved from death.

Dietrich Bonhoeffer

Bonhoeffer was a founder of a Protestant church in Germany that opposed the Nazis. He worked for the resistance, helping German Jews escape to Switzerland. He was executed in 1945 — only a month before the end of the war.

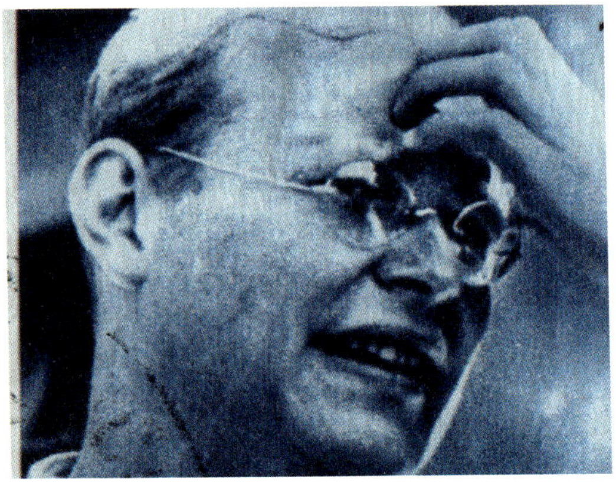

Dietrich Bonhoeffer, 1906-1945

Abbé Pierre, 1912-2007

Abbé Pierre

Abbé Pierre, a French priest, helped Jews to escape from Nazi-occupied France to Switzerland during World War II. Later, he began a movement, Emmaus, to help homeless people. In the winter of 1954, he made a radio broadcast on behalf of those freezing on the streets of Paris.

Timeline of life-savers

1937

Martin Niemoller

German Lutheran pastor who opposed the Nazis is imprisoned for his beliefs.

1941

Maximilian Kolbe

Polish Franciscan friar who sheltered thousands of Jews from Nazi persecution volunteers to die in place of a stranger in Auschwitz concentration camp.

1943

Dietrich Bonhoeffer

German pastor who opposed the Nazis and worked for the resistance is arrested.

1942

Abbé Pierre

French Catholic priest and member of the resistance helps to hide French Jews from the Nazis.

1944

Oskar Schindler

German businessman and member of the Nazi Party composes a list of 1,200 Jews who will work in his new factory, saving their lives.

GLOSSARY

abolitionist One who fights to end slavery.

assassinate To kill someone, especially a public figure.

exile A situation in which someone is forced to leave their home or country to live in another place.

ghetto A section of a European city where Jewish people were once forced to live.

guerrilla Having to do with a type of warfare in which a small group of soldiers makes surprise raids behind enemy lines.

heretic A person who believes or teaches something opposed to accepted beliefs.

tactic A planned action for a particular purpose.

FOR MORE INFORMATION

Jazynka, Kitson. *Harriet Tubman*. London, UK: DK Children, 2019.

Rossiter, Brienna. *The Underground Railroad*. Burnsville, MN: North Star Editions, 2025.

Biography: President Abraham Lincoln
www.ducksters.com/biography/uspresidents/abrahamlincoln.php

INDEX